Through Your Daughter's Eyes

TERI REBHUN

PAGE PUBLISHING, INC.
New York, NY

First originally published by Page Publishing, Inc. 2019

ISBN 978-1-64544-012-3 (Paperback)
ISBN 978-1-64544-015-4 (Digital)

Printed in the United States of America

Dedication

To my children, Erica, Scott, and Sami, who endured and experienced too much too soon for those so young. You gave me the strength and will to go on, for I wanted you to see and feel how precious time can be when you know that is all you have left with someone you love so very much—just time... Just know how proud I am of all of you and how very much I love you. I thank you for loving Grandma like you did and continue to do each day. Keep blowing those kisses upward, and Grandma will always make sure to send them back to the three of you.

For my husband, my love, and my best friend, Bob, how can I ever thank you for being the strength that held me together, for being there if I felt ready to fall, and to love my mother the way you did. I know how very difficult this was for you to experience. Despite it all, you held it together for us all and gave all of yourself through sleepless nights. I can never begin to thank you for your selflessness, patience, and love. I know Mom is your special angel as well.

Thank you, even though that could never be enough. I love you.

Mom, this is for you. We did it. That's such a strange thing for me to say under the circumstances, but we did... or at least I hope this will help ease the pain for so many others. You have helped to make me who I am today, and I will continue to make you proud. You've blessed me with the kind of love like no other, and I only hope I can pass that on to your grandchildren, my children. Just know that you are with me always, it's a power so deep that a part of you will be forever alive within me. Thank you Mom. We had a bond so special that no cancer could ever control. I love you, please know that and take it with you.

Acknowledgments

A special thank you to Dr. Eisen and Peggy at the Cancer Institute, along with Nurse Sue and the rest of the staff. Your never-ending compassion and understanding will stay with me forever. You truly are a special group of people. Thank you from both my mother and myself.

A special thank you to the Nurses and Aids at Compassionate Care Hospice. You were there no matter when or what time I needed to talk or ask for help. It takes a special kind of person to continue to provide the kind of care that you do and ensure that people maintain their own dignity. Thank you for your kindness and devotion to our family. We will never forget you.

It's for all of you
us together
It feels like you're going through it all alone. Just
know that you're not. It takes control of you on all
levels; some of which you never thought existed, until
now. It consumes your entire being, and it can numb
your senses. It's an ache from the inside out, and it
hurts so very bad. With that hurt, as crazy as it may
be, you gather strength with a force you never knew
you had, and with the hurt comes that strength. Keep
it together and focus that energy to keep yourself
sane, together, and in control. For the things you will
see, feel, and experience are truly horrific, and you
must keep both of you focused on tomorrow; you
must try to believe in a tomorrow at all times. Don't
let your loved one down by not believing-as difficult
and insane as it is-there must always be a sunnier,
brighter day-a better tomorrow.

I stare
  how beautiful
  I watch
    your lips
  they move to form sounds
  what sounds
        behind what words
Snoring
      it's a sound but what
  words are behind
        your thoughts
Battles
  going on behind your lids
awakening
        focusing
            listening
                understanding
what comes first
        or next
the battle rages
      keep the mind
        raging
  we don't want it
        at peace.

Heaviness
Sadness
it can grow
so heavy
weighing down
your chest
and
your
mind
Together it can conquer.
Strength, to be uplifted
that is the
mindset
Keep it focused-
don't get off track
Too dangerous
to think
better to float
only sometimes
for you have to fight
always
keep going
never slow down
keep it going

your momentum
Don't sit, don't sleep
or it can swallow you
Keep going, momentum,
keep going…

An inspiration
　you are
to all who know you
　Strength
So very much
　Such fighting
so much of your time
　Such laughter
　from within
　Such kindness
　all around
　you're an
　　aura
　　　of love
for it envelops
　all you know
　and love
all the time
　Keep the strength
　　and the fight
　keep it tight
　　hold it with
　　　strong hands
　don't let it go
　promise
　　you'll never
　　let it
　　　go——-

1/11/00

I sit
  I wait
   I watch
    For what
       I'm not sure
        a sign
         a signal
          or just
            plain hope
It doesn't matter
       really...
As long as it works
       How
       Why
doesn't matter
       As long as it
             works.

As bleak as it may seem to some—
My heart is soaring
   Soaring with hope
      as joyfully
      as the snowflakes
         tenderly swirling
      all around me.

'tis the season
      they say
   maybe so
      hopefully so
we're given another chance
   and we'll take it
      gratefully
         thankfully
      any way
         any time...
   But we have it. We'll
            embrace it.
      Thank you
   thank you so very much.
         Thank you.

We're here again
   Another time
      Same place
different faces
   yet
     same disease
attacks your body
    sometimes your mind
      but never your heart
      or your
         hope
     or dreams
faces masking
   fear
internalizing
   helplessness
screaming out
   yet no one hears
or you
   don't think they do.
Someone near
  can feel your pain
can see your pain
   differently
     maybe so
but feel it no less
  perhaps on a

different plain
a tightness within
my chest
desperately grasping
for hope
wanting to hold
you
so tight
as to ease the throbbing
in your heart
and temples.
Feel the frustration
the unanswered questions
and the anger building
to such a degree
yet not knowing
where to direct it.
Wanting the dreaded disease
to pull through your veins
from your toes out—all out
all away
all gone
feel it flow

let it flow
   out and
      away
away forever
   goodbye
       forever…

3/14/00

Thinking
  Thinking
    Thoughts floating
  thinking
        harder
      even harder
      no answers
        so think
          think harder
  rack your brain
      still no answers
        not fair
        but so what
  still no answers
      roaming thoughts
          hard, double-fisted
        but no answers.
          Never
            any
              answers.

18

Independence
　such an important
　word
　to so many
But it's meaning to you
　that's another story
　a feeling
　　a need
　　　a necessity
for so long
　Don't think you're giving it up—
　Never
as long as your mind
　is in control.
　　Your own space
　　it's there—
　　　you don't know it
　　Just reach out and
　　　grasp it.
　　It's a state of mind
　　　You'll never lose it
　　it's always there
　　Reach out
　　　hold it
　　and you'll see
　　　it's not

the place
not the
    physical place
but
  the mental
    well-being.

A building of brick
  red brick
thousands upon thousands
    of bricks
how long it must have
    taken
    brick by brick
  hour by hour
    day by day
      week by week
       month by month
  was it year after year
  who did this work
    had been given this time
time to build
  a structure
  so solid
    so secure
to endure so many hardships
everlasting
  that's what we want
    time
  a simple word
    4 letters
  so easy to read
  so easy to say

not so unreasonable
a want
a need
a desire
Just plain
want
an ache to continue
to build
to stabilize
to endure
to stand tall.

Your next appointment
  is the 4th they said…
See you then
  the feeling in my heart
    the tears brimming
      in my eyes
How to tell you…
  we're coming back
    the 4^{th…}
Grandma's Birthday
  An omen
    a reason
  the look you had
    the tears brimming
      in your eyes
        this time
together we'll do this
  always together
    we're a team
  and we join hands
    on the 4th
      you'll be even more
        protected…
an aura of love
    and faith
  to keep us coming
    back
  for the next date…

This is all for
        you
My words
    not nearly enough
    but know
        it's my
            heart
my heart
    trying
        desperately
    to connect
        with
            your heart
It's
    for you
my feelings
        my
            thoughts
        all my
            love
    I try so hard
    to connect with
            you
Hoping some of
        my strength
    will flow
        through

you
I close my
eyes and feel
the pull
of my body
gathering the fight
the fight
to pass
through
you
anyhow
anyway
pull it
through my veins
and into
yours...
pressure in my head
to pull it out
feeling so deep
is it ever enough
enough to strengthen
you
heal you
help you
so desperately
wanting
to help you

take the pain
away
so you don't have to
pretend any
more
I know how you
try to hide it
you see
you can't
hide
from
me
I see through
You
I see the
depth
of your inner
struggle
each and
every
day
I see the
effort
the effort it takes
to open your eyes
and know
it will be the

same again today
How very sorry
What an insignificant word
but what else is there
how sorry I can't
can't
make
it
better
can't give you
just one
1
day of that feeling
you most want
the feeling
to
feel good
Just
feel
good
not to feel so
very tired
that it's an effort
yes
an
effort
to swing your

legs over
    the bed
and get up
   up to face
a new
    day
    the days that
change
   the sun that
    may shine
the birds
   that may
    chirp
the crickets
  singing
   in their pond
 the days
   themselves
   that change
and
   you
wanting, needing
to feel that
   change
     too…

but not
　feeling it
　not feeling
　　well enough
　　　good enough
　to join in
　　the cricket's song
not knowing
　when
　　the
　　　time will come
come
　for you
　　to have
　　your
　　chance
　　　to
　　　　change.

4/4/00

Such love and friendship...
   all around you.
It says so much
    for you
     about
       you
encompassing
     a lifetime
  of
    love
     and
      friendship
People...
    friends
  stopping by
    while you sleep
  a private room today
  a cancer clinic
  yet filled with such
    love
     and
      hope
it's trickling through your veins
  does it work
    we just hope
    sit
    and hope

and pray
So many prayers
by so many
friends
Eyes filled with so much
love and caring
and fear
only wanting you
pain free
and smiling
the smile they've known
for so very long
the laughter and
twinkle
that has shone
through your eyes
for so very long
not the glassy
just staring
looking through
you look
but
the natural
easy way
the smile
that's
yours

and
yours
alone...

4/6/00

It's the shots I hate
  sticking, injecting
 burning
    sensations
       I don't want you
    to have to
             feel
Hurting you
    how it makes
          me feel
  I want to take
       away
       the pain
not increase it
    I guess I'm
          helping
but hurting
    just the same
    I'm sorry
    so very sorry
I just want
    to take it
    all away
    and
      I can't
      I hate
       that word

I always thought
it should be
    I can
    I will
    it's not
    happening
    and I'm
    not happy
     I want us to
       be happy
       Smiling
    from the
      heart
      not the
        face
I love you
  know that
  feel that
    embrace that
    for that's a
    wonderful
    sensation
    I want you
only to know
those feelings
not feelings
of hopelessness
  and
      pain.

Look at me
  and
what do you
   see?
Clean scalp
  big dark eyes
   rounded eyes
   like
    your mother
    such depth
Look at me
 and feel the
 loss
 loss of pride
  no
   dignity
     maybe
  a sadness
  looking
   back at me
    eyes so full
    of
    questions
    why
     why
    with no
    answers

no
    answers
for you
    in return
      Again
        I'm sorry
          what other
            words
          no one knows
            yet so
            many
            unanswered
                questions.

I wait for you
  right outside
    I'm right here
    Yet I worry
Are you feeling
      okay
Are you falling
      asleep
  Do you need
    conversation
  Are you up to it
    Probably not
      yet we must
      keep moving
      you'll like
          looking at
          your pretty nails
      give you a
        boost
          feel good
          a little
          jump-start
              maybe
Anything
to see
    you smile
    but

not a lot
　　these days
so we
　　keep on
　　trying
　　you and me
me and you
　together
　　we just
　　　keep trying.

I never found the right moment
        to say
    thank you
            again
I was so overcome with so many
  emotions
It's like a roller coaster ride
    up
        down
        and up again
  can't let your guard down
        always
                remember that.
But thank you
    if my belief has wandered
    you brought me back
    back to a
            reality check.

You've seemed to mellow
since the first time
we met you.
Softened maybe
Could it be
you care?
Really
care
I'd like to think so.
A personal
Interest
that's what makes this
place
special
Caring
nurturing
Your face, what a
nice face today
concerned
I was touched
you'll go through
the slides
and find answers
oh please
find the
answers.

But
  when you do
please
  don't let it be
    the
      wrong
          answers.
So kind
  so full of treating
    and seeing
        sickness
            disease
      what a waste and crime
      what
          a horror
      find the
          right answers
              please...

5/9/00

You want so much
to go home
I really do
understand
you don't think
I do
but my heart
hurts
for you
in what you think
is my
home
but it is
your home too
for as long as
you need it
You'll make
it back
Home
you'll see
and when
you do
it will be
the
right time
for
you

You'll see
  time is on
    your side
  our side
   I may not
    be Sandy
  but
    I'm me
     and
      I'm
       here
        for
        you.

The words
   From your lips
     Help me
2 dreaded words
   little words
with such a
   very
    Big
     meaning.
  Helpless
    that's how I feel
how can I
    help
     you
I would do
   anything
 Anything
   if I only knew
   what
    anything was.
Maybe
  just maybe
   you really
    don't think
  I'm helping

For that
　　I am sorry
　　truly
　　　　sorry
maybe it's the meds
　　　maybe not
just know
　　I would do
　　　　anything
just anything
　if I only
　　knew what
　　　anything
　　　　　was...

5/30/00 & 7/18/00 & 7/24/00

We're here again
my little one
by my side
I hate her seeing the
nightmares
around her
yet she brings such
smiles
to such sad
circumstances.
The little wave of her hand
brings instant smiles,
smiles that light up
unfamiliar
yet very
familiar
sad eyes.
They look for her
that little face
earnestly awaiting
a wave back
or a friendly smile
not a care
in the
world

that's how
    it should be
just continue bringing
    all the joy
       you do
    it's so important
    and oh
       so beautiful
to us
    all.

I feel a scream
    deep within
yearning to come out
    out from the depths
of my soul
    I need—
    we need
      their help—
they know that
    but have
      no answers.
Please
    I beg you
come up with even
    one
small as it may be
 something
   just something.

Don't give up
   don't resign yourself
to knowing
     the unknown.
Please
  together we can
    work through it
  Together
    Only a word to be used
If you're by my side.
  Remember—
  Physically by
  My side.
Together
  we can and we will
  make it through
    Together
Lean on me
  I promise not
    to break
cry on me
  nothing can overflow
  I can
   catch you if you
   start to fall
  I can
  dry your tears
   if they fall

I can and I will
anything
but it must be
together
together for always
we're a team
you and me
Best friends
you and me
Together
with My Mom
by my side.

The whole thing
   it stinks
really stinks
   you know—
you've said
   never
      never
use the word
   hate,
But I do
   Hate
Hate that you
   feel
the way you feel
   Lousy
another great adjective
   it stinks
   all of it
   I hate
     hate
   it
     all.

Terrific
  is the word
    I'd use
for to them
    there is no
      win or lose
The Nurses
    are there
      always there
to give a warm
      smile
      hug and some clues.
Clues to what
    ails you
or makes you feel
                blue.
Clues to bring you
    up and hopefully
      feeling better
  yes
    that's true.
Such
    warmth
such
    compassion
such
    true

```
        devotion
it all
  emanates
     from each
        and every
one of
        you.
Thank you
     just isn't enough.
Hope you know
     that it's all meant
        meant
           from the heart.
```

I lie awake
  filled with
    anticipation
awaiting your
      return
It was supposed
  to be
    such a
    nice trip
the sights
  the fun
  you could
    most would
  say
     wonderful
but I
  knew
knew it would be
  very difficult
    for you…
Don't they see
  how hard you're
trying
    to have that
  fun
and enjoy
  those sights…

A body
  racked with
     pain
a pain felt
   so deep
  I'm feeling it
     with you.
How do we keep
        fighting

Remember

    How do we not…

We saw you on
  on the wedding video
Your granddaughter
  said
  you look like a doll
  yes—
  a porcelain doll
   so very beautiful
  so very
     fragile
you glided
  like a swan
  head
   held high
pain hidden
  behind your
   trusting and medicated
    eyes—
  but
   so
    very
     beautiful
   and so
   very strong—
  a fragile
   porcelain
    doll

barely
   held together
yet
   such an
    unbelievable
    strength
from within
   un
    break
     able...

Well
we knew it
  knew it
  in our
    hearts
    the news
    it wasn't
    what we
      wanted
    to hear
    we braced
        ourselves
I had my
  security
    my little one
    to hold on to
  you had
    me
  you always will
    our eyes
      met
      and
          locked
  we
    knew
    together
      we knew

think about
        the next step
            they said—
there's
        no thinking
        we can
            never say
        what if...
            we're in
                it together
            all the
                way
                for the
                    long haul
                together
                    we can
                        conquer all
        because
            our love
                is stronger
        than
            any
                disgusting
            yet oh so powerful
            hideous
                    disease.

It started
  and
    you're
     oh
       so brave
it's your own
    private torture
you say
    I can't feel it
not like you
      that's true
but I do feel
        it
deep,
          deep within
a pain so deep
in my heart
  it hurts
    it churns
    it's eating me
      chewing away
        piece
            by
                piece
yes it hurts
a different pain
    but—

```
              pain
just the same
       I want to
       take it
              away
       from you
and
       I can't
       that's a
              pain
              you can't feel
though it's not
              true
you have
       felt that pain
                 too.
Not so very
       long ago—
but
   that's my
          personal hell
          and you
          felt
              that too.
```

It's not easy
  watching you
spacing out
    sometimes
it's not easy
  taking a
    double take
not knowing
    how to respond
it's not easy
  watching you
    look through
      me
    lost in space
    not knowing
    what you're
      thinking
who you may
    be seeing
  far away
    Help me
      to see through
      your eyes
  so you can
    know

that I
    feel
       too.
It's not easy
    making you
       feel
    that I
       feel
         too.

We did it
    again
we made it through
    again
you did great
    the doctor said
one, two, three—
    it's in—
and we'll be
 out
 on our way
    again
together
    going home.

The leaves are falling
    Please
don't you fall too
The battle gets tougher
    we'll fight it harder
Our heads get cloudier
    we'll have to
        clear them
our hearts
    get heavier
how do we fight that?

I hold you in my arms
  oh so delicately
 what I really
      want
 is to hold you
 oh so very tight
  and I want
       you
  to hold and
     hug me back
oh so
        tight
I want to feel you
in my mind
      forever
 I miss
   your hugs
 you know what...
       I
     miss
           you.

I must be missing
   something
   this dreadful disease
   there must be a place,
a Doctor,
  some help
  some miracle
  somewhere.
  But who
   and what
    and where
  and of course
   the answer
    no one gives
     why?

The Nurses are here now
    from
        Hospice Care
It's really so unfair
    and it's so hard to bear.

I'm not ready to give up;
   I can't imagine anything
    without you.
   My head is so foggy
   I just can't sleep,
    My heart is so heavy
   it will never be
          the same.
I want you with me
        Always.
How can I keep you
     protect you from
       the evil, hideous thing
that's overtaking you?
I know you're fighting
  you're so brave
  but hurting
     so badly
  you ask for
     God's help,
  my help
    where is it?
  It seems so
   out, far out
 of my reach.
 I need to catch it
 hold on to it

envelop you
in it.
I can't let you down
Please God,
now it's
my turn
help me
not to
let
her
down.

Your love to so many of us was a precious stone—a pearl which had so much meaning to you. It's flawless just like your loving, giving heart. Your love had no bounds—you brought more joy to us all than words could ever express. As a Mother, there is no better word than love; as a Grandmother—you are a hero and as a Friend—you could never be replaced.

But knowing you as we do—you wouldn't want heavy hearts. We really need to see through the darkness and celebrate your life. Because no matter what path life took you—you kept your head high to overcome any obstacles that got in your way. No matter how bad a hand you were dealt—you never said a bad word—you tried to find the good. I always said you were a better person than me. You were forgiving—you tried desperately not to harbor any resentment. You've taught me how to feel good, how to express love and kindness, and to be myself and be proud of that. I only hope I can instill what you've always given me in Erica, Scott, and Samantha. I want to feel the love you've always felt and be the kind of friend you've always been. You are a hero to us all, as well as a, Best friend.

I feel as if my heart wants to explode because no matter how desperately I search for words, there truly are none. You are in every way, beautiful inside and out.

You've brought laughter ringing through our home, and more happiness than anyone could imagine. You've always kept our family, the "Tabakin Bunch" together, and have always been so proud to brag about eleven grandchildren.

You've been an inspiration to Bob and I, for you and Sandy showed us the beauty in marriage, and for that we're thankful that we can keep your Anniversary alive with happiness and smiles.

I feel so empty, broken, and so very sad, yet at the same time I feel so very lucky and so complete. You fill up my heart, and I know you'll live within me and I within you forever.

Alan and I as well as all of us today are truly blessed. Blessed with the knowledge that you've touched our lives in a way no other could. You've guided us to be our own person, make our own decisions, and stood by us, wrong or right. If we needed to fall, you were there to catch us—if we held our heads high, you straightened our shoulders to lift even higher. You are an inspiration and a joy to all.

You are and always will be my very special, very Best friend.

I love you.
Please take that with you.

Laura
10/2/38—11/29/00

I can't sleep
 I can't think
  my heart aches
I see and feel you
   all around me
  you're there
    but not
      here
   with me
     my special friend
   it hurts so
     no one
      no one
     could possibly
        understand
     the pain
   I try to hold it
     under
        control
     but I feel
       so torn up
     into
       pieces
     tiny
        pieces
      that

can't
can't
be
mended
be strong
that's how
I should be
so you
could rest
easy
is that why
you were afraid
to go—
I'm
strong
stronger
with
you
but you
left
not
wanting
to
but
you
did
and I
ache
so bad
so much
so hard

did I tell
    you
how much
    it
      hurts
how
    much
        I miss you

We tried
  I tried
but was it
  enough
 no
  I guess
    not
      we couldn't
       didn't
      save you
  what
     what
    did I miss
     so much
        exhaustion
    did I see
      through
          it
    lying there
    next to
        you
    did I come up
      with
        answers
        no
         I guess
            not.

I need that hug
  that one
    only you
      could give me
the true warmth
  the love
    only you had
      no strings attached
        pure
          real
          a mother's love
            my Best friend
            both are
                gone
                how very sad
I miss them
  both of them
  so very much
    it will
      never
        never
      be
        the same
      ever
        ever
            again.

I need to
  complete
our book
    but
where
does it
  begin
and why
    must
    it
    end?
I guess
  an ending
  was not
  how
      I wanted it to be.

You're now
   the brightest star
   our shining star
with points
   up
no longer
   down
you twinkle in
   the moonlight
you twinkle in
   the sunlight
      you smile
       for
      you're at peace
      smiling down
            on me
            on us
Rest easy
   my
      darling Mother
   my very
      special
            friend.

Almost a whole year has passed, and no matter what they say, it never gets any easier.

I yearn for your smile, the one that appeared so easily, the laugh that burst out and engulfed your face and was so very contagious, your hugs that were yours and yours alone.

I try so hard to feel your arms around me. I hear your voice, and I still find myself talking to you, asking what would you do? What do you think?

I always wanted to be the kind of person you were—but I've come to realize—no one can, no one ever will be.

You lit up our lives with love, with hope, with special understanding and a warmth and compassion beyond words.

I have a perpetual ache that never seems to ease. Just know that all of us miss you terribly, love you from the depths of our souls, and be confident knowing you live within us always.

I love you Mom.

It's been a while
   quite some time actually
   since I've picked up a pen.
I know you want to see me smile and be carefree to
some degree...
I hear you talk to me, but it never seems enough.
You've shown me a sign—
              but I don't feel it's enough.
I guess I never will—
Selfish I am. I want you back but I want you to rest
easy—not having to worry
              peaceful
holding hands with the one you love most—
that's the image I always see—
         hands clasped,
         warm smiles,
      loving words passed from your
      eyes and back again.
Always love and a longing for life...
   I want to accomplish this for you—
      I will—
      I'll always keep going—I'll never
      let you down or
         me—
     we're still a team
     Always.

A blanket of snow
covering you
I was so afraid
you would be
   so so
    cold
    closing my eyes
I hear the
   calm
   I'm no longer
     afraid
    you're cold
    it's a warm
    blanket
a blanket
 of white
  soft
   snow
   lying ever
so gently
 embracing
 you
 in peace.

I sit here
 and I wait
wait for what
   I'm not sure
Just sure
   that I wait
but only
     silence
Sure
   there are
       signs
 sometimes
   never often enough
   Silence
     yet such screaming
       screaming
       within
       I can't let go
       not true
       I guess I can
           do
             anything
       but
         choose
             not to

Loneliness
    I have so much to say
but
  you're not
      here
      to listen
        not really
          anyway
Time
  it goes by
   each day
     so
       quickly
   it goes by
    but you
      you
    don't
      come back
  I have to get
  it
  get it through
   my
     head
   you're not
     not

coming back
but
then again
I know you've
never really
left
you live inside
inside
my heart
always
and
forever.

Okay—
  it's time now
time to
  let go.
 I promised myself
 for you and
     me
   that I'd finish
  this
    complete this
       for us
       since we
         can't
       do it
          together
       it's for
          you
       for
        so many
        who
          have
            loved
              and
                lost
              and
          continue
              loving

it's
  come to an
        end
this is it
  I have to make
    closure
this has to be the way
    for me this time
I need
need
  to
      let go
      not of you
          never
            of you
      just
        let go
          you know
        I feel
        it's time
          to let
          go
smile
  see the world
    the birds
    the blue sky
    really see

open my eyes
be happy
be grateful
for all I do have
and for having you
open my
heart
open my
mind
let go
let it
out
all of it
let it go
this has to be
the end
it is
the end
of this
chapter anyway—

I have more
hopefully
so much
more
and many
more
chapters ahead

I need to explore
and fill
so much more
to learn
to see
to share
you've taught me this
by giving
so much
of yourself
all of you
to so many
all of
us
want to
thank
you
thank you
for saying inside
of myself
it's time
time
to close

end the story
of pain
go on with
life
and
the
living

I love you.

It will be six years
   Six years
so hard to imagine
   I look out over the ocean
waves crashing
   yet soothing
   and I think how much
you loved and truly enjoyed
   the sound
    the sun
     the peacefulness
      of the sand and surf
How far have the heavens engulfed you
   Not a day goes by that
      I ache
       for you
    to be living and smiling
     and loving your surroundings
     your family
       your friends
       your
         daughter
A perpetual ache—
     I've said that a lot
    Aisles of Mother's Day Cards
    I can no longer buy

Birthday cards for you,
            no longer
Special friend with
      Mother and Daughter
            I can only remember
Beautiful memories
      Lodged deep,
deep within my heart
forever sealed
      yet never, no never
            forgotten
   We...
      you and me
         had such a special bond
no words could capture
      only love
   Just know my love is
from yesterday, is today, and
will be forever tomorrows.

         I love you Mom
         I miss you Mom
            Rest peacefully Mom

I still can't believe you're gone
but never from my heart and soul.

About the Author

Teri has been writing since she can remember. It has taken her years, but with the encouragement of her wonderful husband and children, Teri has finally been able to "let go" and release this book which is so dear to her heart. She hopes this will help others who are experiencing the same heartbreak that Teri, herself, has felt. It is so important to her that others understand that it is okay to share your true feelings with so many others who have and continue to fight alongside a loved one due to this deadly disease.

Teri is a graduate of Emerson College in Boston, Massachusetts. She donates her time on a committee to help raise funds and awareness for the Cancer Support Group in her community. Teri loves to read, cook, entertain family and friends, and jump in the pool for a swim as often as weather permits! Teri's pride and joy are her three grown children. She lives in New Jersey with her loving husband and adorable dog, Lexi.

CPSIA information can be obtained
at www.ICGtesting.com
Printed in the USA
FSHW021256130819
60975FS